How Hattie Hated
Kindness

Margot Sunderland

Illustrated by

Nicky Armstrong

Speechmark

Speechmark Publishing Ltd
Telford Road, Bicester, Oxon OX26 4LQ, UK
www.speechmark.net

Once, there was a little girl called Hattie who lived on an island.

Hattie liked everything hard and spiky.

She liked sharks and crabs, and stinging centipedes.
She liked anything that bit.

One day, some little boats sailed on to Hattie's island.
"Hello Hattie, we've brought you some lovely music,"
they said.

"GO AWAY!" screamed Hattie, and she made a big, blustery wind to blow the boats away.

The next day an aeroplane flew in.
"Hello Hattie, we've brought you some little dolls to
play with."

"GO AWAY!" yelled Hattie,
and she sank the aeroplane.

The day after that some people built a bridge to Hattie's island. "Hello Hattie, we've brought soft pillows and cosy rugs for you to sleep on."

"BE GONE!" shouted Hattie, exploding the bridge with a rocket she had made that morning.

The day after that, some seagulls dropped by to ask
Hattie if she would like to go fishing with them.

"FLYING SMELLIES!" screamed Hattie, spitting and
kicking as she tried to pull their wings off.

And after that, they all stopped coming to the island.
They all stopped coming to see Hattie.

Hattie was terribly, terribly, all by herself.

"Oh no," thought Hattie. "I didn't really mean to push them all away. It just felt good doing all that smashing and spoiling."

Feeling horrible, Hattie sat down by the water's edge
on a particularly hard and spiky rock.

She thought and thought.

"How has it got like this?" she asked herself. "How come I hate soft and want hard? How come I hate kind and choose cruel? How come I hate beauty and like ugly? How come I hate love and love hate? I must be a very bad girl indeed."

Now, the lapping water-over-her-toes heard what Hattie was saying. "Hattie is not bad, she is just very hurt," it lapped gently.

Hattie sneered, "Stupid little lapping. Be a raging, angry sea. Rush and swirl and crash against the rocks!" She tried to kick the water with an enormous kick, but it didn't seem to have any effect whatsoever.

The water-over-her-toes went on, "If your life had
been full of kind people, flowers and birds and gentle
loving things, you wouldn't have wanted all this
hardness and hate. It is so difficult to stay warm in a
cold, hard world."

Hattie had a dim memory of what the water-over-her-toes was saying. A dim memory that she had once been a very sad and frightened little thing in a too hard world. She had had to become hard, so the fear and awful pain would go away.

"But I am not brave enough to be gentle," she said sadly. "I will help you," replied the water-over-her toes.

So each day Hattie sat on the hard and spiky rock and let the water lap over her toes.

And each day, she began to feel a little warmer and calmer inside. And each day she knew more about a gentler world.

After a while, she left the hard and spiky rock, and went to sit on a sunny sand-dune instead.

Then one day a crab with very large pincers crawled up to Hattie and gave her a tiny white shell.

"I used to be an angry biter," it said, "but then the gentle water lapped over me."

Hattie and the crab became great friends, swapping shells and stones and multi-coloured seaweed . . . as well as the occasional friendly nip, of course!

Then after that, Hattie started to build a bridge to the warm and cosy world across the water.

And all of the people on the shore waved hello.

"Hello Hattie!"

A Pea Called Mildred
Margot Sunderland

A Wibble Called Bipley
(and a few Honks)
Margot Sunderland

Ruby and the Rubbish Bin

Teenie Weenie in a Too Big World
Sunderland

Willy and the Wobbly House
Margot Sunderland
Illustrated by
Nicky Armstrong

How Hattie Hated Kindness
Margot Sunderland
Illustrated by
Nicky Armstrong

The Frog who Longed for the Moon to Smile
Margot Sunderland
Illustrated by
Nicky Armstrong

A Nifflenoo Called Nevermind
Margot Sunderland
Illustrated by
Nicky Armstrong

The Day the Sea Went Out and Never Came Back
Margot Sunderland
Illustrated by
Nicky Armstrong

Speechmark

Speechmark Publishing Ltd
Telford Road, Bicester, Oxon OX26 4LQ, UK
www.speechmark.net

ISBN 0-86388-461-X

9 780863 884610